Understanding Prophetic EVENTS - *2000* - PLUS!

EARNESTLY CONTENDING

I0170061

for the State of ISRAEL

END TIMES - *SERIES TWO*

DR. ALAN PATEMAN
Foreword by Dr. Ron Charles

By Dr. Alan Pateman

BY DR. JENNIFER PATEMAN

AVAILABLE FROM APMI PUBLICATIONS, AMAZON.COM AND OTHER RETAIL OUTLETS

EARNESTLY CONTENDING

for the State of ISRAEL

DR. ALAN PATEMAN

BOOK TITLE:
Earnestly Contending for the State of Israel,
Understanding Prophetic EVENTS-2000-PLUS!

WRITTEN BY Dr. ALAN PATEMAN
ISBN: 978-1-909132-71-9
eBook ISBN: 978-1-909132-72-6

Written in 1996, Released in (Copyright) 2018 Alan Pateman

Published By:
APMI Publications
In Partnership with Truth for the Journey Books **26**
Email: publications@alanpateman.com
www.AlanPatemanMinistries.com

Acknowledgements:
Author/Design/Senior Editor/Publisher: Apostle Dr. Alan Pateman
Editing/Proofreading/Research: Dr. Jennifer Pateman
Computer Administration/Office Manager: Dr. Dorothea Struhlik
Cover Image Credit: © NomadSoul1, www.fotosearch.com

Unless otherwise indicated, all scriptural quotations are from the HOLY BIBLE, NEW INTERNATIONAL VERSION ®. NIV ®. Copyright © 1973, 1978, 1984 by the International Bible Society. Used by permission of Zondervan Publishing House. All rights reserved.

Where scriptures appear with special emphasis (in bold, italic or underlined) we have edited them ourselves in order to bring focused attention within the context of this subject being taught.

❖

Dedication

I lovingly dedicate this book to the Jewish people. In opening our eyes to the truth about the Jews and the Jewish people in regard to the Christian World, the Nations and the End Times, we will attempt through these pages to discover that truth and final out come for their destiny and ours. I pray that the Holy Spirit will give you insight into this very often misunderstood reality.

❖

Table of Contents

❖

Foreword

*Eschatology — the study of
the current knowledge of the End-Times**

In our modern society, the word invokes mental images of The Mark of the Beast, Tribulation, Armageddon and the last war to end all wars, and Final Judgment.

Although it has only been in the past 100 years that the word, *eschatology*, has been used as a noun to identify events that deal with the end-times or the time that immediately precedes the end of all things as we know it, teachings

*Note: This Foreword by Dr. Ron Charles is included in all four parts of this End Times Series *(Series One: Israel, the Question of Ownership; Series Two: Earnestly Contending for the State of Israel; Series Three: The Temple, Antichrist and the New World Order; Series Four: The Antichrist, Rapture and the Battle of Armageddon).*

11

associated with the event, theories proposed to predict the event and philosophies, *(both religious and non-religious),* developed that attempts to explain or clarify the event dating back thousands of years.

The ancient Egyptians taught that the end of the world or the end of all ages, as they called it, would first be preceded by a great apostasy against their historical gods and then a massive return to the worship of the gods just before the end came.

The Assyrians believed that the end will be preceded by a great war on the plains of the Euphrates River between the armies of the West and the armies of the East and that at the height of the war, the sun god would appear bringing eternal peace and punishment to evil ones.

The Babylonians believed that the end will be preceded by a great leader who would cause all people to worship him, as the reincarnated Marduk. Then, when he had firmly established himself as Marduk, that Marduk himself will come and judge and destroy with intense fire, all those who were deceived by the great leader.

In fact, we now know that in virtually all developed societies for the past 5,000 years, from Egypt to Rome and from Assyria to Persia, there has been a belief by those societies that there will indeed be an end to all things and that this will be accompanied by wars and natural tragedies, judgement of all people, rewards for the believing benevolent and righteous, and punishments for the evil and or non-believers.

As it has been for thousands of years, so it is in our society today, with but one major exception—the Jews. It was in the early-19th century in England that a handful of theologians and bible teachers began to dissect the scriptures and discovered what they felt to be a uniform thread of God's compassion and benevolent consistency in dealing with the descendants of Abraham, that stretched throughout the bible from Genesis to Revelation; maintaining its constancy through wars, exile, natural disasters, genocide, and societal extermination.

This belief began to crystallize into a theological position that spread throughout Europe, into America and throughout the world, until by the mid-19th century it had become the accepted doctrine more than the exception in European and American evangelical and fundamental religious circles.

As this doctrine became more accepted in the late 19th century, eschatology specialists began to see how God's dealing with the children of Abraham over the past centuries and the horrors that they were forced to endure, has in fact set the stage for the modern development of the state of national Israel, which in turn is recognized as God's physical end-times epitome whereby these approaching events can more readily be recognized and chronicled.

Dr. Alan Pateman's four part End Times Series (*Series One: Israel, the Question of Ownership; Series Two: Earnestly Contending for the State of Israel; Series Three: The Temple, Antichrist and the New World Order; Series Four: The Antichrist, Rapture and the Battle of Armageddon*), not only seeks to bring the reader *"up to date"* with regard to present day societal eschatological convictions, showing how Israel is in fact, God's chosen instrument that will be used to chart and to instigate fulfilment of these long anticipated end-time events.

He also accurately traces the history of how the Jews through history have been used as God's instrument; how evil forces have for centuries, all the way up to this present time, sought to destroy these people, their mission, their purpose, and their unique position within the overall plan of God; and how the worldwide entrenchment of modern day apostasy, materialism and deception will immediately proceed the realization of these end-times events, anticipated for so many thousands of years.

Such a work has long been needed that successfully marries the past, especially that of the Jews and of the rise of anti-Semitism, with the events of the future, and clarifies the mysteries of eschatology so that those of us who await the glorious return of our Lord Jesus, can more easily understand and appreciate the inimitability of the exceptional days and times in which we live — the End Times.

Dr. Ron Charles
The Cubit Foundation
www.cubitfoundation.org

❖

Preface

In the year of 1996 my wife and I and our small son lived in the Tuscany area of Italy for the period of nine months. *(This is the duration of time before we moved to Italy in the year 1999).* And up to this time I had been preaching frequently throughout Europe, Africa and America etc., with a measure of success.

One would say that these early years of ministry were powerful and brought me in touch with many wonderful men and women throughout the nations. But one of the most difficult and evading revelations was the whole subject on

*Note: This Preface is included in all four parts of this End Times Series *(Series One: Israel, the Question of Ownership; Series Two: Earnestly Contending for the State of Israel; Series Three: The Temple, Antichrist and the New World Order; Series Four: The Antichrist, Rapture and the Battle of Armageddon).*

the End Times. I'd been to bible school and been successful in ministry yet I did not really have an understanding or should I say *any* understanding about the Jews, the Babylonian structure, the rapture etc.

Then one evening as it became seemingly my custom to read to my family and anyone else who *(team members etc.)* was there in the evenings. I would read from a particular book that God had inspired me to pick up or to take from my shelf. And it was then on one of those quiet, yet warm summer evenings in '96 that I began reading the biography written by Derek Prince, the husband of *(then his first wife)* Lydia Prince. The book was titled *"Appointment in Jerusalem."*

Oh, What a Wonderful Book that Is

I've cried as I've read the pages - as the Holy Spirit touched my own heart - my journey in ministry seemingly has similarities to this story - being led by the Holy Spirit along a life journey to fulfil the call of God. Her journey was to Jerusalem. My journey is to the nations. But wherever God is leading us, He always leads us by his Holy Spirit and we can learn through similarities, not only through the scriptures but also through the testimonies of others and of course the biographies that have been put into writing.

Let me make a statement here, the Holy Spirit is our teacher and He knows what we need to learn or teach us at any given time. Therefore I only read the books or listen to the tapes that He has led me to listen to or read that particular day. He knows what needs to be built into my soul and spirit man - He knows what I need to be fed upon to nourish my very being, He always knows what's up ahead as He's the one that's leading us.

But coming to a place of reading the whole of this special book, *"Appointment in Jerusalem"* God began to speak to me about the End Times. As I picked up a pen and began to make a few notes, I felt the Holy Spirit tell me to get up at 6 o'clock the next morning and begin a time of study because He wanted to reveal to me His plan for the End Times.

Six Weeks in God's Study

Every morning for the next six weeks I got up and the only place that was very quiet where I would not be disturbed was in a garage in the basement of our apartment block. Every morning I would be down there at 6 o'clock praying, studying and writing. Day after day, sometimes for hours at a time or until I felt a release and I knew that the day had finished and a new day would begin tomorrow.

Only there was a woman in the garage next door who had a big knitting machine, which she used to sit at most of the time. At first it used to disturb me with the noise of the thrashing back and forth of her machine! We never met, I never saw what she accomplished in her knitting over those weeks and she would not have had a clue that God Almighty was visiting one of His sons to reveal revelation on a very important subject that most Christians know nothing about.

Six weeks went past and what you have in this four part series on the End Times, *(Series One: Israel, the Question of Ownership; Series Two: Earnestly Contending for the State of Israel; Series Three: The Temple, Antichrist and the New World*

Order; Series Four: The Antichrist, Rapture and the Battle of Armageddon - also incorporated as five course syllabuses within the teaching curriculum of the LICU University) is a result of that time.

I can honestly say that this insight, understanding, revelation and impartation has changed my life. I have such a heart for the Jewish people, for Jerusalem as a Capital of Israel and for what God has in store for this time.

Of course you need to read and ask God to reveal to you by His Spirit, His truth. And together I pray with the same desire as Lydia Prince and ask you and every Christian to pray for Jerusalem.

> Lydia wrote *"I suddenly came to see that we Christians have a debt that has gone unpaid for many centuries – to Israel and to Jerusalem. It is to them that we owe the bible, the prophets, the apostles, the Saviour Himself. For far too long we have forgotten this debt, but now the time has come for us to begin repaying it – and there are two ways that we can do this.*
>
> *First, we need to repent of our sins against Israel: at best, our lack of gratitude and concern, at worst, our open contempt and persecution.*
>
> *Then, out of true love and concern, we must pray as the psalmist tells us, 'for the peace of Jerusalem,' remembering that peace can only come to Jerusalem as Israel turns back to God. God has shown me that from now on to pray in this way for Jerusalem will be the highest form of service that I can render Him."*[1]

❖

CHAPTER 1

The Church Age Begins

Fathers and the Root

Bob Walker in 1952 prophesied, "that the Assemblies of God and other Pentecostals had planted the seeds of a mighty 'Charismatic' revival." He stated that soon the revival would break out in all denominations. **It has come to pass.** We are now seeing the end-time outpouring of the Spirit.

Satan is raging. We are at war. But the prophet said, *that when the enemy comes in like a flood the Spirit of God will raise up a standard against him (Isaiah 59:19).*

One of the greatest dangers facing the Evangelicals, Pentecostals and Charismatics is a rejection of our biblical heritage and radical changes of our views on the End Times. The non-Kingdomists and Dominionists are examples of this.

New and extreme winds of doctrine seem to blow around us with gale force. Nevertheless many stand firm and proclaim God's truth for these last days. Indeed, we are *"set for the defence of the gospel"* and shall *"earnestly contend for the faith."*

After Jesus' death and resurrection came the Day of Pentecost, the Holy Spirit was poured out and the Church was born.

Tensions between Jew and Gentile

The Church grew, thousands of Jews believed that Jesus of Nazareth was the Messiah, and that His death and resurrection was exactly what the prophets had foretold. Many went out as Jesus had commanded them *(Matthew 28:19)*, Go into all the nations. The result was that even Gentiles were professing Jesus Christ as their Lord. Questions arose among Jewish believers about whether the Gentile believers were required to keep the Mosaic Law or not?

Tensions grew between Jewish and Gentile Christians, which led early to each side, having to define in great discussion their relationship regarding both the Law and circumcision. The Gentile believers should simply abstain from certain kinds of food, such as blood and from fornication *(Acts 15)*.

For the Jews both the Abrahamic and the Mosaic covenants had the same validity, and it was unthinkable to interpret history with its promises in an allegorical or spiritual manner.

Neither Jesus nor the Apostles denied the historical testimony of the Old Testament but they gave its texts an added perspective. Paul described the Non-Jewish believers as branches, taken from a wild fruitless olive tree *(the heathen nations)*, and grafted into cultivated, fruitful olive tree with a nourishing sap filled root *(Israel)*.

> *If some of the branches have been broken off, and you, though a wild olive shoot, have been grafted in among the others and now share in the nourishing sap from the olive root, do not boast over those branches. If you do, consider this: You do not support the root, but the root supports you.*
>
> *(Romans 11:17-18)*

Warning to the Gentile Church

Despite Paul's explicit warning to the Gentile churches not to boast against the *"Fathers"* and the *"root,"* i.e. the Jewish people, it was not long before the official Church developed the theology that God had completely rejected *"old Israel"* and replaced it with the *"Church."* All the promises in the Old Testament were taken to mean the *"Church"* in the capacity of *"the new Israel."*

Greek Gnosticism secured a foothold in the Church, by means of various rites, as did Babylonian mystery cults. Struggles for power by certain bishops also had an effect, as well as local superstitions. Then in the fourth century the Roman Caesar Constantine, declared that the struggle against Christianity was lost. So he proclaimed religious freedom throughout the Roman Empire and Christianity was declared the official religion.

The Religious World Opposes Revival

The Church became an institution for authoritarian politics, this in turn developed into the Roman Catholic and Greek Orthodox religions we know today. Religion, supremacy, legends, superstitions and human traditions gained power, but Christianity gradually disappeared. Mariology and veneration of saints came increasingly to the forefront within society. This seemingly brought a twofold development that led an assault against bible-based revival movements and against Jews.

After Christianity was accepted by the State, it became distorted. Doctrines on grace, faith, repentance and salvation were perverted. Repentance from the heart and the new birth were no longer emphasised. People believed that God's grace was obtained through the sacrament — infant baptism, communion, confirmation, confession, marriage, priesthood, ordination, and finally, extreme unction.

It was said you could only become a Christian by doing all these things! The most sacred was infant baptism. It was taught that an infant was born again through water baptism, as God's Spirit was imparted through the water. Then as the child grew and participated in the various sacraments within the church system, then the child was a Christian.

Assurance of salvation was lost, the result, an erroneous doctrine of works, which combined various occult elements. The forming of *"holy orders"* and *"holy places"* with *"holy objects,"* *"saints."* All these were nothing more than man's contrived attempts to reach God and obtain His approval.

Many superstitions began to flourish together with the worship of saints, fetishes, fables, myths and unbiblical traditions. Biblical revelation was lost and withheld from ordinary people who were lost in a maze of condemnatory fabrications and superstitious beliefs.

Liturgy, Pilgrimages and Flagellation

Holy lifestyles and reverence for God were lost and replaced by liturgy, pilgrimages, flagellation, monks and holy orders. Candles and crucifixes became holy objects. Icons became an occult medium through which it was said, life and grace were imparted from heaven. As the papacy developed so too did the worship of saints *(ancestor worship)*, and Mariology. Latin became a holy language and the liturgy was read with Latin prayers like occult incantation.

Religion had now taken over, New Testament Christianity had lost its power extinguished by demonic imitation. The life had gone; two particular groups targeted, inspired by demonic powers and led a twofold assault, one against bible-based revival movements and the other, against the Jews.

❖

CHAPTER 2

Replacement Theology

Becoming Increasingly Prevalent

Unbiblical features became part of the norm as the Church moved away from its Jewish and biblical roots. As Christianity was proclaimed the official religion of the Roman Empire: becoming legal requirement, replacement theology became increasingly prevalent.

A false charge has echoed from this time, with lasting accusation, the Jews are still being charged with the same violent attacks. This accusation is the most serious because it has theological root. *Did the Jews murder Jesus?*

Augustine *(AD354 to AD430)* systematically developed, *"Kingdom Now Theology."* He did this with reference to the theology of the Kingdom of God, applying this to the Jewish thinking about themselves as God's Kingdom.

Augustine developed the thought that their dispersion *(the Jews)* was a sign to Christians who when they saw what had befallen the Jewish people who had rejected and murdered Jesus, their own Messiah. This then would be a warning concerning what would happen to anyone falling away from the Church — the *"Mother"* of all believers.

He also argues that the Church's interpretations of the Old Testament injunctions are shadows. He maintains that these shadows become realities in the new life Christ gives! Declaring that the Old Testament is a prophecy concerning Christ, and therefore Christians now possess all the promises contained therein. The application is that the *"Church"* is in itself an institution, and the *"Heavenly State"* to be — set up on earth.

Condemned to Fugitive Status

Furthermore all Jews were condemned to fugitive status, vagabonds wandering the earth as punishment for putting to death Christ. This fever had now spread the excitement of a fight and being in good stead for it was a new phenomenon. The theologians and so-called church fathers who were to be examples, Christ like, were also involved and quick to embrace anti-Semitism.

Because of the anti-Semitic view many people shut the Jews out, unless of course they became Christians like everyone else. Some treated this as a new fad, meaning that everyone else was *"doing it,"* like the latest fashion. The question was and is: *Did the Jews murder Jesus? Was it justifiably, biblical?*

Let's find out.

First: The Roman authorities sentenced Him to death and the Roman soldiers carried out the execution. According to history both Romans and Jews were involved, so to be consistent all Romans and Italians and Jews ought to be persecuted.

Second: Theologically speaking Jesus was to be the Lamb who would be sacrificed for the sins of all mankind. Sinners then killed Him! Jesus repeatedly told His disciples that He had to go to Jerusalem to suffer and die there.

Much earlier John the Baptist had prophesied over Him saying, "Look, the Lamb of God, who takes away the sin of the world" *(John 1:29)*. When Peter tried to defend Jesus' life with a sword in Gethsemane,

Jesus declared:

> *Do you think I cannot call on my Father, and he will at once put at my disposal more than twelve legions of angels? But how then would the scriptures be fulfilled that say it must happen in this way?*
>
> *(Matthew 26:53-54)*

Jesus also said:

> *The reason my Father loves me is that I lay down my life — only to take it up again. No one takes it from me, but*

I lay it down of my own accord. I have authority to lay it down and authority to pick it up again. This command I received from my Father.

(John 10:17-18)

Third: Is there any room for hatred towards the Jews? The bible says in 1 Corinthians 13:5 that Love...Keeps no record of wrongs. Persecution, personal hatred, revenge has no place in a believer's heart. The Jews are not eternally damned; God loves them as He does the entire world. **The Jewish people will always be in God's plan.**

When you pass through the waters, I will be with you; and when you pass through the rivers, they will not sweep over you. When you walk through the fire, you will not be burned; the flames will not set you ablaze.

(Isaiah 43:2)

Since you are precious and honoured in my sight, and because I love you, I will give men in exchange for you, and people in exchange for your life. Do not be afraid, for I am with you; I will bring your children from the east and gather you from the west.

(Isaiah 43:4-5)

I ask then: Did God reject his people? By no means! I am an Israelite myself, a descendant of Abraham, from the tribe of Benjamin. God did not reject his people, whom he foreknew. Don't you know what the scripture says in the passage about Elijah – how he appealed to God against Israel?

(Romans 11:1-2)

I believe the question is answered,
No one took the life of Jesus!
"He gave it."

CHAPTER 3

Babylonian Captivity of the Church

Religions of the World Persecute the Jews

The backslidden church, mainly the state religious churches *(The Church of England, The Roman Catholic Church, The Lutheran Church etc.)* have stolen and imitated what God had given to both the Jewish people and the living Church, clothing herself with wealth. Luther described this as the, *"Babylonian captivity of the Church."*

As the authority of the Catholic Church became more and more powerful and fused with that of the state, laws were passed to humiliate and oppress the Jews.

All proselytising was not allowed, and the right to own Christian slaves was also prohibited. Mixed marriage was considered a criminal infringement on public morals and worst of all, in order to meet the theological demand that the Jewish people should be subordinate to Christians, Jews were banned from public office.

The law penetrated to the very core of human rights, making it difficult for a Jew to be faithful to his beliefs, and to tempt him to convert to Christianity.[1]

Persecution and Public Flogging

Even though the Roman Empire was crumbling, the Church continued tightening its hold on the political powers in those countries which embraced Catholicism. Even those Jews who had become Christians under pressure, because of threat of persecution, were treated as second class citizens. In Spain it is said they were being publicly flogged, and from the records of the 17th contention at Toledo we can read the following:

"Seeing it is common knowledge that the Jewish people, because of their blasphemy in its very worst form, are defiled, and by their spilling of the blood of Christ, stained, and through their infamous practices, soiled, it is fitting that they should bewail a grave and severe punishment suited to the number of crimes...

Our pious and God-fearing king Egika, kindled by the fires of the holy faith, not only desires to requite the disgrace suffered by the cross of Christ but also, determined to penalize, with all severity, the intentions of the Jews to bring destruction upon his people and native country, commands that all their property be confiscated and their assets be turned over to the public treasury.

Those infidels themselves, together with their wives, sons and other offspring should be banished from their dwellings to be permanently scattered into Spain's every province, in lifelong servitude, waiting upon them to whom they shall be entrusted...

We likewise decree, that their children of both genders, from their seventh year, may no longer reside with their parents nor have any contact with them. The gentlemen who take them in, shall see that they be fostered by very reliable Christians so that the men marry Christian women and the women in like manner be wedded to Christian men.

Neither the parents nor their children shall under any circumstances be given opportunity to observe the customs of the Jewish cult or in any other way be allowed to persist in their belief."[2]

Crusades Against the Jews

On the 27th of November 1095, Pope Urban II *(1088-1099)* gave an order for a crusade against the Jews on the home front. Incensed mobs broke loose and violence erupted. Some Jews escaped their executioners by fleeing, others it said preferred to take their own lives rather than fall into the hands of the murders.

Then a second crusade, with the cross as their emblem, whipped up by church leaders, massacred entire Jewish communities in Europe and Russia; it was an assault on the Jews. Fighting those who were *"enemies of the Christian faith."* Hatred further fired up these so-called Christian believers when Abbot Peter de Cluny made the following statement:

"But what gain is it if we seek out and oppose the enemies of the Christian faith in distant lands while these lecherous and blasphemous Jews, who are far worse than the Saracens *(Moslems)* not in remote countries but here in the midst of us, go unpunished while so audaciously and recklessly blaspheming Christ and all the Christian sacraments.

If Saracens are to be detested, who, even as we, confess that Christ was born of a virgin and in much concerning Him agree with us, though denying His godhead and that He is the Son of God... and cast doubt upon His death and resurrection..., how much more are the Jews to be loathed and hated which wholly deny Christ and the Christian faith and who reject, blaspheme and mock the virgin birth as they do all the sacraments which are given for the salvation of mankind?

I do not say this to sharpen the king's or Christians' swords against the Jews... God does not want them to be *'entirely exterminated,'* but to be kept unto worse torment and shame, like the murderer Cain, to a life which is worse than death."[3]

Pope Innocent III and the Fourth Lateran Conciliate *(1215)* had a decisive effect upon the laws of the church concerning the Jews.

Council Opposes the Jews

"The council opposes the Jews and their alleged usury. *(By law, Jews were not allowed to practice normal crafts or middle-class professions in society, which forced them to support themselves by trading and money lending).* Jews must clothe themselves in a way, which distinguishes them from Christians. In this way the isolation of the Jews began, which resulted in establishment of the ghettos from the end of the 15th century. Jews who have converted to Christianity should at all costs be hindered from reverting to the Faith of their Fathers."[4]

The Catholic Church went through a dark chapter in history in their aggression towards the Jews. Arguing or justifying cannot excuse the Catholic Church, if as it was said that the priests and theologians were deceived by barbaric spirits of the time, leaves one wondering about the rest of their theology!

The Harlot Church

Some have thought that the Roman Catholic Church is the harlot church where the Antichrist will rule, and the city of Babylon being Rome, Italy. The Harlot is not any single denominational structure. She is an amalgamation of all the world's ecclesiastical, man-made religions, including the present day denominations choosing to have only a form of godliness.

Today the ancient harlot is about to receive a new vehicle through which she can function. Quite possibly it is the World Council of Churches, which works for the unity of all religions. While man-made religions are working to bring all Christians under their control, the Holy Spirit is working to bring them together as the Glorious Church!

It is possible that the city destroyed at mid-Tribulation will be the headquarters of the harlot religious system, or as some have identified it, the world church. But its exact identity is unknown. Presently it is Geneva, Switzerland, headquarters of the World Council of Churches, World Bank centre, and city of treaties between nations.

Grant R. Jeffrey, who is internationally recognised as an outstanding prophecy teacher says in his book, *"Prince of Darkness"* that; "In a fascinating revelation, Archbishop Runcie of the Church of England told Time Magazine *(October 16, 1989)* that he had given a special ring to the Roman Pontiff. He explained that this ring was *'an engagement ring'* between him and Pope John Paul II as a promise of the coming union between the Church of England and the Church of Rome.

Removed Supernaturally

These ecumenical groups have often complained that the only real obstacle to their religious union was the resistance of the evangelical conservative Christians. Once these Christians are <u>removed</u> supernaturally by the rapture, there most probably will be little resistance from any other group to its proposed union.

Ultimately this false world religion will involve an alliance of the Roman Catholic Church, the Russian and Greek Orthodox Churches, various Protestant groups, and New Age cult groups. Virtually all religiously minded people will enthusiastically join this false church in a tremendous alliance with the new political leader of the New World Order, the Antichrist." *(I think Evangelical Alliance – E.A. – needs to be careful that it does not fall into this trap).*

"The prophet John saw this future satanically inspired alliance of religion and politics as symbolised by the Babylon, **'Mother of Harlots.'** As John prophetically looked down the centuries he saw this worldwide religious system supporting the Antichrist and the ten nations of his kingdom in their rise to power:

> *I saw a woman sitting upon a scarlet beast which was full of names of blasphemy, having seven heads and ten horns. The woman was arrayed in purple and scarlet, and adorned with gold and precious stones having in her hand a golden cup full of abominations and filthiness of her fornication. And on her forehead a name was written:*

> *MYSTERY, BABYLON THE GREAT, THE MOTHER OF HARLOTS AND ABOMINATIONS OF THE EARTH.*
>
> *(Revelation 17:3-5 NKJV)*

Note that John saw the End Time false religious system *'sitting upon a scarlet beast.'* This indicates that the religious system will initially be lifted up and honored by the Antichrist's political allies. However, John reveals that this last day religious system will be characterised by apostasy and blasphemy. She will be known for her vast riches, yet her true secret nature is indicated by the prophet's words, *'abominations and filthiness of her fornication.'*

Spiritual Apostasy

The bible often uses the imagery of sexual unfaithfulness to signify spiritual apostasy. This false church will wallow in sensuality and will express the materialistic spirit of these last days. It will be known as *'Mystery, Babylon the Great'* because it will secretly embody the Babylonian religious mysteries that have characterized every man-made religion and cult since man's rebellion at the Tower of Babel."[5]

Is Time Running Out?

Is time running out? Soviet leader Mikhail Gorbachev, and Pope John Paul II, whatever next! *"This is the Holy Father,"* said Soviet leader Mikhail Gorbachev, introducing his host to his wife, Raisa. *"We are aware we are dealing with the highest religious authority of the world, who is of Slavic origin as well."* To which a smiling John Paul II replied: *"Yes, I'm the first Slavic Pope, but I'm sure providence prepared the way for this meeting with Mr. Gorbachev — and Mrs. Gorbachev as well."*

Thus concluded the historic summit at the Vatican, signalling a dramatic reversal of relations between the Soviet Union and the Roman Catholic Church.

"As tokens of their unprecedented visit, the Gorbachevs gave the Pope two 14th century books written in Church Slavonic, the language of the Russian Orthodox liturgy. From the Pope, Rasia received a mother-of-pearl rosary.

For the leader of the Communist Party and the Soviet chief of state there was an early Christian mosaic of St. Peter's tomb with a relief of Christ. It bares a scriptural message in

Latin, one that Gorbachev may have recognised from his Christian childhood: *'I am the way, the truth and the light. All those who believe in me shall live.'"*[6]

❖

CHAPTER 4

Replacement Theology Produces Anti-Semitism

Martin Luther Protests

We know that Replacement Theology is prevalent in all Christian groups to some degree. But to one man's experience it became too much to bear — Martin Luther *(1483-1546)*. Luther protested about Replacement Theology by nailing a 95-page thesis to the church door at Castle Church, Wittenberg, on 31st October 1517.

The veil was lifted when he received a revelation on Romans 1:16-17, like a flashing light.

I am not ashamed of the gospel, because it is the power of God for the salvation of everyone who believes: first for the

Jew, then for the Gentile. For in the gospel a righteousness from God is revealed, a righteousness that is by faith from first to last.

He realised that righteousness, peace, justification and mercy were not earned through man's efforts or religious deeds. God imparts them through Christ's sacrifice on the cross. Everything He has done for us on the cross, He works in us when we received Christ Jesus. *"For we maintain that a man is justified by faith apart from observing the Law"* (Romans 3:28).

Up to this point in his life he was a Roman Catholic, a monk, with all its teachings on works, superstitions, human traditions and church politics. Doctrines on grace, faith, repentance and salvation were perverted. Repentance from the heart and New birth was no longer emphasised. People believed that God's grace was obtained through the sacraments — infant baptism, communion, confirmation, confession, and priesthood.

The Search for Truth

Luther a monk, then priest, and later Professor of Theology, was hoping to find peace with God through all his good works, but the opposite was true. He religiously fasted and prayed to Mary and the saints. He wore horsehair shirts, made regular confessions and pilgrimages, and bought indulgences hoping to find peace with God. But it was seemingly futile.

During this period Luther visited Rome, Christianity's religious capital. He staunchly prayed, fasted and gave alms.

He even walked on his knees praying on Sancta Scala. He did everything in his power to please God, yet he remained empty inside.

When he gradually became aware that the whole religious system to which he belonged was absolute, he intended to reform it. He began to realise that the Church had totally perverted the gospel. Legalistic works had replaced the gospel of grace; faith had been substituted by superstition and religious actions.

Human legends, traditions and the Canon Law had replaced the bible. Instead of the outworking of the Word and the Spirit through ministerial gifts, there were Popes, Cardinals and Priests whose word took precedence over the bible.

Selling indulgences was particularly loathsome to Luther. The Church taught that monks and priests could be paid to pray for the souls of the dead. The Pope at the time, proclaimed a special indulgence called *"Peter's penny"* which was used to build St. Peter's in Rome.

This money, recovered through this indulgence, was supposedly to save your relative years of suffering in purgatory.

The Reformation is Born

The reformation is born! The grip of Catholicism over Europe was giving way to this restoration of teaching. And Luther was excommunicated and out-lowed by the Catholic Church.

Luther who God had used and was diligent in his cause also fell into *"Replacement Theology."* Like the Catholic theologians, Luther had interpreted all the promises of salvation in the Old Testament as fulfilled in Christ. The belief in salvation, which the Old Testament saints held, is what is known as ***"anticipated belief in Christ."***

In other words, the Christian Church is also anticipated in the Old Testament. This is true and in accordance with the witness of the New Testament but if one by reasons thinks that the role of the Jews in God's plan of salvation is concluded, then one is *"walking in darkness and does not know where one is going."*

Luther's Anti-Jewish Teaching

Postulations of the Anti-Jewish kind by Luther, once fuelled the Catholic Church in its persecution of the Jews, can be summed up as follows:

- God's judgmental wrath abides upon unbelievers and He alone can annul it. God Himself has appointed the Jews to judgement as punishment for what they did to His Son Jesus

- Jews cannot repent of their own free will. There is no way in which they can be brought into the church; they are stiff-necked unbelievers and incurable despite all efforts to help them

- Their continual blasphemy of Christ and God proves their religions to be still alive but hostile toward God

- This appointed suffering abides likewise upon other enemies of Christ and God. The Israelites' rejection of Christ is constantly being repeated within Christianity, and the Jews personify the belief, which is perpetually breaking out within the Church[1]

Bitter controversy was the result of three connected writings produced by Luther in 1542-1543.

He wrote, "A man who doesn't know the devil may well wonder why the Jews above all others, are so hostile towards Christians. Moreover, they are so without cause, for we show them all goodness. They live here among us and have the use of our land, streets and lanes while our leaders are still sitting back, snoring open-mouthed, allowing them to lift from their purses and coffers, and to steal and rob them as they fancy.

How? By allowing their own subjects and themselves to be fleeced and impoverished by the usury of the Jews, and so, with their own money, they make themselves beggars."

Proposals to Evangelicals

Luther in giving proposals to Evangelical leaders of the day said, *"They dishonour God and worship the devil when they, in their blasphemous fables, make Christ out to be a witch-doctor."* And all the atrocities which had been ascribed to the Jews such as poisoning water, child-stealing, blood-guiltiness were probably true.

He suggested that the Jewish houses should be demolished and the occupants removed to temporary huts built by gypsies. Their right to safe-conduct should be abolished, prohibition of usury, slave labour for able-bodied Jews and Jewesses and the burning of all synagogues and Jewish schools.

Thankfully there was some sanity among those Evangelical leaders, one cannot help thinking where the Love of Christ was, where Luther was concerned!

History's worst Anti-Semite

The Jews account Luther as one of history's worst anti-Semites. They consider him as one who laid the foundation for the extermination of the Jews during the Second World War.

Through the preaching of the clergy, the church was not only compliant with, but in many cases supportive of, anti-Jewish tendencies in the Third Reich. One of Hitler's leading men, Streichner defended the extermination of the Jews at the Nuremberg trials by quoting from Martin Luther's writings!

In conjunction with the celebration of Luther's 500th anniversary, the Lutheran World Council issued the following statement:

"We Lutherans can neither accept nor overlook the vehement verbal assaults made by the Reformer upon the Jews... Luther's sinful anti-Jewish statements and his fierce attack upon the Jewish people must be acknowledged with deep sorrow.

All possibility of similar aggression, both now and in the future, must be removed from our churches."

❖

CHAPTER 5

Jewish Migrants
are Waving the Flag

They Are Coming Home

The Jewish people are, and will continue to be God's people, He has not forgotten them or ever changed His mind where they are concerned. Remember His covenant is everlasting.

This is what the Lord says,

> *He who appoints the sun to shine by day, who decrees the moon and stars to shine by night, who stirs up the sea so that its waves roar – the Lord Almighty is his name: "Only if these decrees vanish from my sight," declares the Lord, "will the descendants of Israel ever cease to be a nation before me."*
>
> *(Jeremiah 31:35-36)*

Nowhere in the New Testament is the Church called Israel and yet, Israel and the Israelites are mentioned seventy-seven times. The Jewish people, Israel, are the Jewish people and the Church is the Church.

And now His people are Coming Home from all over the world, *the time has come for the flag of Israel to be waved by the Jewish migrants* who are gathering in their promised nation of Israel, today.

> *Then the Lord your God will restore your fortunes and have compassion on you and gather you again from all the nations where he scattered you. Even if you have been banished to the most distant land under the heavens, from there the Lord your God will gather you and bring you back.*
>
> *(Deuteronomy 30:3-4)*

Everlasting Covenants

God's covenants and promises to His people are everlasting. God loves His people with an everlasting love, we see this in Jeremiah 31:3 where He says, *"I have loved you with an everlasting love; I have drawn you with loving-kindness."*

Now in the midst of present chaos in the Middle East God is re-establishing His people, against all the odds and conflict, − no force on earth will ever succeed in doing final harm to God's chosen people! God has declared His divine protection upon this nation *(Ezekiel 36:7-12)*.

This rebirth of Israel has taken place and now that blue and white Star of David is coming from such diverse places as Russia and Ethiopia. These precious people, the Jews, are flowing into Israel by the thousands, fulfilling the End Time miracle migration.

> *He will set up a banner for the nations, and will assemble the outcasts of Israel, and gather together the dispersed of Judah from the Four Corners of the earth.*
> *(Isaiah 11:12 NKJV)*

The world looks on, with eyes of mixed feelings, the very existence of Israel is a mystery; it seems impossible that such a tiny nation can draw so much attention from around the world. Can Israel exist in the midst of so much opposition from so many fronts? Thousands of Palestinians have been held captive in Israel in an attempt to stop internal terrorism from erupting beyond its already volatile state.

The Palestine Liberation Army wants Israel destroyed, regardless of what different peacekeeping committees are saying. Many of the Arab countries surrounding Israel want to see that tiny nation eradicated. Yet, Israel is surviving — and will continue to survive — **because it is vital to End Time spiritual history.**

Christ Predicted

F.S. Copleston says in his book, *"Jesus Christ or Mohammed?"* that Jesus predicted before His Second Coming a representative number of the nation would have returned to the land and been re-established as an independent nation. These prophecies are necessarily involved in warning His disciples among those returned representatives of the nation that when they saw the abomination which makes desolate *(the image of himself which the coming Antichrist will set up in the rebuilt Temple)* to flee to the mountains *(Matthew 24:15-22)*.[1]

Daniel refers to this image in chapter 12:11, and in chapter 9:27 to his causing the Levitical offerings, which will then have been re-established, to cease, that he alone be worshipped as God *(see also 2 Thessalonians 2:1-4; Revelation 13:11-17)*.

Christ also referred to the seven years covenant Antichrist will make with Israel in saying: *"I am come in my Father's name, and ye receive Me not: if another shall come in his own name, him ye will receive" (John 5:43 KJV)*.

Jerusalem the Capital

But in order for the Jews to rebuild the Temple it would be necessary for them to possess the whole city of Jerusalem, east as well as west, though it contained the Mosque of Omar, a site most sacred to Muslim. In their last war with the Arab League, despite the whole might of the Muslim world against them, they took it in fulfilment of these bible prophecies, and have retained it despite the utmost pressure by all other nations to persuade them to hand east Jerusalem back to the Arabs.

Their refusal has so annoyed these nations that they have all withdrawn their ambassadors from Jerusalem in protest, but without avail, because as Mr. Begin said, ***"God has given it to us, and we will never give it back."***

But Christians who understand these prophecies, and God's purposes to save Israel and make her the channel of His blessing to all nations in the Kingdom Christ will establish at His second coming, have established a Christian Embassy in Jerusalem. Twenty-four nations have sent Christians as ambassadors there. In 1988, four thousand Christians led the Jewish procession at the Feast of Tabernacles.

Christ also predicted that among those who would have returned to the land covenanted to them through the unconditional Abrahamic covenant would be some who believed in Him as Messiah, and who would be persecuted by the Orthodox just prior to His return *(Matthew 10:23)*.

There are a number of believers in Him now among those who have returned, and are being persecuted.

❖

CHAPTER 6

The Rise of Modern Zionism

The Rebirth of the State of Israel

To quote Dr. Kac's book, *"The Rebirth of the State of Israel:"* Throughout the many years of great Dispersion the Jews never forgot Zion. The return to Zion was their consuming passion. Their whole life was conditioned by the conviction and hope of their eventual return to the land of their forefathers.[1]

> *If I forget thee, O Jerusalem, let my right hand forget her cunning. If I do not remember thee, let my tongue cleave to the roof of my mouth; if I prefer not Jerusalem above my chief joy.*
>
> *(Psalms 137:5-6 KJV)*

A definite change in mood came with the ushering in of the Era of Emancipation towards the middle of the eighteenth century, which marks the end of the middle ages for the Jews, when the degradation of European Jewry reached its worst.

It was the cumulative effect of centres of inhuman oppression. From this time on there began a general improvement in the condition of Europe's Jews, and within one century the Jews of Central and Western Europe became emancipated, receiving in some countries full civic and political equality.

European Jewish Affairs

This new turn in affairs of the European Jews was the outgrowth of profound changes which had taken place in the world in the preceding two centuries, brought about by the extensive geographical discoveries, by the Protestant Reformation, and by the French and American Revolutions. In the religious sphere these events spelled religious liberty.

Organised religion was deprived of the power of the support of the state in enforcing its particular brand of belief. Religious faith was to be based on the religious conviction of the believer, rather than on blind obedience to external authority. The emphasis in religious matters was shifted from the masses to the individual.

The effects of the political emancipation on Jewish life was far-reaching. One of these goes under the name of *"Assimilation."* This is a relatively new term in the Jewish vocabulary, and it denotes a process by which the Jew strives to become fully integrated into and identified with the political, economic and cultural life of his non-Jewish surroundings.

The changed political and economic conditions in Europe, and the removal of the Jewish civic and political disabilities, encouraged the Jew to leave his Ghetto isolation and enter into the general stream of life of the country of his residence.

He began to dress like the Gentiles, speak their language, attend their schools, and mix and mingle with them. He renounced his Jewish tradition, deserted the Jewish schools, and became part and parcel of his Gentile environment.

Jews Slower Tempo

This development first began in Central and Western Europe and from there it spread to Eastern Europe. There it preceded at a slower pace due to the greater concentration of Jews in that area and the slower tempo with which the progressive ideas of Western Europe seeped into Eastern European countries.

The Jew ceased to look upon himself as an alien in a foreign land, and began to consider himself a member of the nation of the country of his birth or adoption. The word *"exile"* began to lose its meaning, and the age-long dream of a return to Palestine lost hold of its grip upon the Jewish mind. The country of his domicile was now his Zion.

These changes in legal status, language, occupation, and education of the Jew were beginning to affect also his attitudes toward his religion. His departure from the Ghetto surroundings often meant a departure from the faith and world outlook of traditional Judaism. With many Jews this change in attitude meant a complete break with Judaism. Intermarriages and baptisms made deep in-roads into the Jewish communities of the emancipated countries.

"There was hardly a Jew of any standing in Berlin at the beginning of the nineteenth century who adhered to his inherited faith." In the nineteenth century about 205,000 Jews adopted Christianity over the world. In Hungary over 12,000 Jews were baptised in the 1919-1929 period. In the beginning of the twentieth century many Jews in Germany and Austria left the Jewish community without affiliating with any other religious community.

This loss of *"Jewishness"* by the Jews afforded full civic and political rights in the countries of their emancipation, their desire to be recognised only as citizens of the country of their domicile or birth, would have completely defeated God's purpose in making them His covenant people. Had they been allowed to have these desires fulfilled it would have prevented the fulfilment of the very many Old Testament prophecies, and Christ's prophecies also, of their return to the land and re-establishment as an independent nation in that land.

The Assimilation Movement

In order to appreciate the seemingly insuperable obstacles which stood in the way of our Lord's *(and Old Testament)* prophecies, concerning their return to the land being fulfilled, it has been necessary to refer to this *"Assimilation Movement"* among the emancipated Jews of Europe, and note how God overcame them all.

The process of emancipation of the Jews in Germany was in the space of one generation. In an incredibly short space of time, many Jews whose parents had been born in ghetto surroundings, had risen to places of distinction in all walks of life. This included science, art, literature and politics, which had hardly been completed when a wave of new Jew-hatred struck in the last quarter of the nineteenth century and in time overflowed to countries outside Germany.

Dr. Kac says, that German national pride and jealousy at the Jews' pre-eminence in ability in all walks of life provoked a most hostile reaction in that nation of anti-Semitism, and was followed by similar outbreaks of anti-Semitism in Russia and France in particular.[2]

Thus the Foundation was laid for the anti-Semitism of German Nazism of the twentieth century which led to the extermination of the bulk of European Jewry in World War Two.

The rise of modern Zionism was the result of this rise in anti-Semitism in the nations of Europe.

❖

CHAPTER 7

Moses Hess the Activist

His Collaboration with Karl Marx

The greatest contribution to the development of the modern Zionist movement was made by the activities of Moses Hess and Rabbi Zevi Hirsch Kalisher.

Hess was born in Germany of Orthodox parents in 1812. In his younger days he broke away from the tenets of traditional Judaism and became absorbed in the intellectual activities of the Germany of that day. For a time, he collaborated with Karl Marx but was not happy with Marx's materialist conception of history, and broke with him in the end.

Much as Hess recognised the importance of social conditions for social ideas, he considered it essential that socialism should not be based on economical and technical development alone.

For him social freedom is either a result of spiritual freedom, or it is without a foundation and turns over into its opposite. He saw the heart of the social problem of his time as proceeding — not from the needs of the stomach — but from the needs of the heart, and from ideas.

Hess Belonged to the Dispersed

Already in 1840, some twenty-two years before the production of his "Rome and Jerusalem," Hess began to experience a change of heart about the destiny of the Jewish people. The false murder accusation in Damascus in 1840 — the so-called Damascus Affair — was the immediate cause of Hess's change of attitude towards his people.

The effect of this *affair* was to pour out a feeling of dismay and agony into the hearts of European Jews. *"Then,"* Hess declares, *"it dawned upon me for the first time, in the midst of my socialistic activities, that I belong to my unfortunate, slandered and dispersed people."*

In "Rome and Jerusalem," written in 1862, and in his other utterances, he analysed the unique position and destiny of the Jewish people. And laid down a program for the rebirth of Israel, and its restoration in Palestine along lines in which the modern Zionist movement, born some thirty years later has been proceeding ever since. Hess's thoughts on the subject of Israel's national rebirth were as follows:

- The Jewish people and Palestine are inseparable
- The national rebirth of the Jewish people is impossible without a return to the soil of, and full normalisation of Jewish life, in Palestine
- The ultimate aim of the Jewish national rebirth is the setting up on earth of the Messianic Kingdom of God, but this cannot take place until the Jewish people have regained first their national State of Palestine
- Hess predicated the founding of Jewish colonies in Palestine, when the time became ripe, "under the protection of the great powers of Europe"
- The founding of Jewish settlements in Palestine will be preceded by the acquisition of land, which land should be the common possession of the Jewish people
- The establishment of societies for agriculture, industry and commerce in accordance with the principles of the Mosaic Law
- The revival of the Hebrew language in Palestine

He also spoke with great significance of the restored State of Israel as a link between East and West. It is remarkable how much of this program of the Zionist movement has been fulfilled exactly as foreseen by Hess.

Rabbi Kalisher's Efforts

The significance of Rabbi Kalisher's efforts on behalf of the modern Zionist movement lies in a different direction. He was a highly educated Rabbi, born in the German part of what was originally a Polish province. He was steeped in Rabbinic law and secular subjects.

The importance of Rabbi Kalisher's Zionist activities is seen in the effect of his labours on Orthodox Judaism. Orthodox Judaism clung to the belief that the restoration of the Jewish people to the land of their forefathers will take place only through the agency of the Messiah. For Jews to try and rebuild Palestine by themselves was considered by Orthodox Jews as forcing the issue before the appointed time, and therefore bound to fail.

The tragic way in which the many pseudo-Messianic movements of the past had ended may have strengthened Orthodox Judaism in this belief.

Pioneers Prepared the Way

Rabbi Kalisher set out to break this passive, defeatist attitude of his orthodox brethren. In his writings he sought to prove from the bible and Rabbinical sources that not only is it God's will that the Jews should re-establish themselves in their ancient Homeland. But that the Messiah would not come until the Jews had prepared the way for Him by rebuilding the land to which He is to come.

Rabbi Kalisher pointed out that there are to be two returns to Palestine, the first to consist of a small group of pioneers who will prepare the way for a later return of the whole nation.

In consequence of the many years of self-sacrificing work on the part of this venerable and deeply religious

Rabbi, *a new spirit of hope and labour was breathed into the dormant body of a people hibernating through the centuries of persecution in the hollow log of tradition and faith!*

Three external events were the immediate precursors of the birth of the modern Zionist movement:

- The resurgence of the spirit of Jew-hatred in Germany under the name of radical anti-Semitism

- Intimately associated with this event was the renewal of anti-Jewish policies in Russia, which culminated in the pogrom of 1882

- The plot against the Jews in France, which was one of the underlying factors of the Dreyfus Affair in 1894

Theodor Herzl in Paris

The insecurity and essential abnormality of the Jewish position on the modern world impressed themselves deeply on Theodor Herzl, a Viennese Jew, during the trail of Captain Dreyfus in Paris, in which he covered as a correspondent for the "Neue Freie Presse."

Herzl became convinced that the only solution for the centuries-old sufferings of the Jewish people is its reconstitution in a country of its own. In 1897 he published his *"Judenstaat" (The Jewish State),* in which he gave expression to his convictions, and laid down a plan for the re-establishment of the Jews as an independent nation.

In what country Jewish national existence should be organised did not interest Herzl at the beginning of his labours on behalf of the Jewish people. But the violent opposition, which arose to the Uganda project of Britain, soon convinced Herzl that the Jewish people would never consent to the establishment of the Jewish State in any country but Palestine.

The Manifesto of Zionism

The book by Theodor Herzl, *"Der Judenstaat" (The Jewish State),* which was to become the manifesto of modern Zionism, was the compilation of dreams of many a Jew, and a trumpet call to Zion.

On August 29, 1897, delegations from sixteen countries met in Basel, Switzerland, for the first Zionist Congress. Afterward, Herzl wrote in his diary: *"I created the Jewish State in Basel. If I said so out loud today, I'd be laughed at everywhere. Maybe in five years, but in any case fifty, everyone will know it."*

This publication of Herzl's book and the directness, clarity, precision and daring manner in which he dealt with the whole problem of the Jews, stirred the whole Jewish people from one end of the world to the other.

Congress formed the Zionist Organisation

When Herzl convinced the Congress in Basel, Switzerland, to consider the project, Congress formed the Zionist Organisation.

Zionism strives to create for the Jewish people a home in Palestine, secured by public law. The Congress contemplates the following means to attain this end:

- The promotion on suitable lines of the colonisation of Palestine by Jewish agricultural and industrial workers

- The organization and binding together of the whole of Jewry and means of appropriate institutions, local and international, in accordance with the laws of each country

- The strengthening and fostering of Jewish national sentiment and consciousness

- Preparatory steps towards government consent where necessary to the attainment of the aims of Zionism[1]

Thus political Zionism was born. It made articulate the millennial Jewish hopes and aspirations for a restored Zion. It brought the whole question out into the open and laid it at the doorstep of the Gentile world.

Since the world did not want the *"Jew in the midst,"* it was up to the same Gentile world to help the Jew find a place in the world, and this place is none other than Palestine.

❖

CHAPTER 8

The Balfour Declaration

A National Home in Palestine

World War One freed Palestine from Turkey. In 1917, twenty years after the first Zionist Congress, the British Government issued the Balfour Declaration in which it solemnly promised to assist the Jews to secure a National Home in Palestine.

The Declaration becomes the basis of the British Mandate over Palestine under the League of Nations, ratified separately by the United States Government. *Thus America and the nations belonging to the League of Nations guaranteed the rebuilding of Jewish Palestine.*

(At this time, the land of Israel was part of the Ottoman Empire, ruled by the Turks. However, the British fought the Turks

in the Middle East during the First World War, and took Jerusalem, under General Allenby, and the Turks lost Palestine).

Political Zionism encountered some opposition from certain Jewish segments. The assimilationists, denying the whole idea of a Jewish nation, were afraid it would provide the anti-Semites with more fuel for their anti-Jewish activities on the ground of Jewish disloyalty to the countries of their domicile.

Socialists and Nationalism

The Jewish socialists were against Zionism because they were against all nationalism. Orthodox Jews were against it for the reason already discussed above. But the events between the two World Wars, especially the destruction of European Jewry by Nazism, have practically wiped out all opposition to Zionism within Jewry. Assimilationism, Orthodox Judaism, Socialism — all failed.

Zionism became the unifying factor and the rallying point for all Jewry, and in **May 1948, the centuries old dream of a restored Zion became a reality with the reconstitution of the State of Israel.**

This document provided legal status to the Jews' endeavours to return to their ancient homeland. As described in the Balfour Declaration, Palestine was an extensive mandate, or area, including both Israel and Jordan as they are today. In other words, the whole of this area was intended to become a national home for the Jews.

Lord Balfour on the 3rd November 1917 made the following declaration in Parliament: **"The British Government views with favour the establishment of a National Home in Palestine for the Jews."** Perhaps this was the result of an invaluable service rendered to the Allied cause in World War One by Dr. Weizmann, a Jewish chemist in Manchester University *(England)*, who had entered Britain from Russia before the war.

Threatened with defeat through shortage of munitions, while German submarines sank vessels and threatened the few supplies that were left, the British Government asked Dr. Weizmann if he could produce a munitions formula from plentifully available materials. This probably contributed to anti-Semitism under Hitler.

Nuremberg Decrees

In Germany, when Hitler came to power in 1933, he issued the Nuremberg decrees, which denied German Jews any legal or citizen rights.

They became harassed and many were arrested, which led to many murders. Nazis worked feverishly, showing their true face as the Second World War gained momentum.

Jews were gathered together, **Nazism was becoming increasingly seen for what it was, an organised satanic power with a plan to totally annihilate all of the European Jews.**

They were forced into concentration camps such as Auschwitz, Sobibor and Dachau, and murdering them by this time by the thousands.

When the world became aware of what was the worst outrage in world history, *(the holocaust)* there then was a basis for the creation of a Jewish state in Palestine. The survivors wanted to NOW GO HOME, to go to their ancient homeland. The Jews who had immigrated earlier, and lived in the Palestinian Mandate during the Second World War, worked intensely.

Immigration because of Persecution

They wanted their brothers home, and also to get the world to acknowledge the need for a *Jewish National Home,* as promised by the Balfour Declaration. But other events had to take place to make the Balfour Mandate possible.

This involved Turkey, who had been in alliance with Britain and France since the Crimean War of 1854, yet broke the alliance in order to join Germany when in the early days of the war everything pointed to a German victory.

Another problem was of course of Arab Nationalism, they could not tolerate the arrangement described in the Balfour Declaration, and put pressure on the British government to break its promise.

❖

CHAPTER 9

Mohammed was not a True Prophet

Even the Koran says the Land is Theirs!

Since Moses was a prophet who made many predictions, verified by history, Christ's claim to be the Prophet like unto Moses *(John 5:45-47; Luke 24:24-27,44-47)* is likewise verified.

As we have seen in the fulfilment of His prophecies concerning His Church and the Gospel and the nation of Israel, which refutes the claim of Mohammed and his followers that he who did not make any true prophecies, was this prophet. The following extract from the Koran has a vital relativity to the confirmation of *"God's Chosen People"* in the land of Israel:

THE KORAN SAYS: ISRAEL IS GOD'S CHOSEN PEOPLE, AND THE LAND IS THEIRS.

Sura *"The Table"* v23-29: "And remember when Moses said to his people, *'O my people!'* I call to mind the goodness of God towards you when He appointed prophets among you, and appointed you Kings, and gave you what you had never been given before, to any human beings: Enter O my people! The holy land, which God hath destined for you. Turn not back, lest ye be overthrown to your ruin.

They said *'O Moses!'* Therein are men of might, and verily we can by no means enter till they have gone forth. **But if they will go forth from it, then verily we will enter in.**

Then said two men of these who feared the Lord and to whom God had been gracious, 'Enter in upon them by the gate: and when ye enter in it, ye overcome! If ye be believers put your trust in God!'

They said, 'O my Lord! Verily of none am I master but of myself and my brother: put thou therefore a difference between us and this ungodly people.'"

Sura *"Al Araf"* v134-137: "And we brought the children of Israel across the sea, and they came to a people who gave themselves up to their idols. They said *'O Moses! Make us a god; make us a god as they have gods.'* He said *'verily, ye are an ignorant people: for the worship they practice will be destroyed, and that which they do is vain.'* He said *'Shall I seek any other god for you than God, when 'tis He who hath preferred you above all other peoples?'"*

The Question of Israel's Rights

This must infallibly settle the question of Israel's right to her present possession of the land says, F.S. Copleston, for every Muslim who truly believes the Koran is God's revelation of His Will. The trouble is, as many professing Christians reject any doctrine of the bible, which they do not agree with and yet still think it makes no difference to their being Christians; likewise very many Muslims reject every doctrine of the Koran they do not agree with, and yet still think it makes no difference to their being true Muslims.

The Iran-Iraq war would have been impossible if all those who supported it really believed the Koran to be God's revelation, for it says:

"But whosoever shall kill a believer of set purpose, his recompense shall be hell; forever shall he abide in it, God shall be wrathful to him, and shall curse him, and shall get ready for him a great torment" *(Sura Women, v95).*

They break the Law forbidding usury by saying that investments are not usury, and so claim to believe in the Koran as God's word.

Behind Arab Hostility

In the book of Daniel, spirit powers tried to stop Angel Gabriel as he was on his way to answer Daniel, who was in prayer.

Then the prince of the Persian kingdom resisted me twenty-one days.

(Daniel 10:13)

The same spirit powers are active today, hindering the Jewish people from returning home; for it is there in Israel that they will fulfil their calling. Every year the Muslims have a month of fasting, Ramadan. All over the world *(remember Arabs surround Israel)*, the last day of the fast is ended by spells and curses being uttered against the State of Israel.

Every Muslim is programmed, indoctrinated with prejudices, they are incited to an ecstatic hatred, and it has to be said not just towards the Jews but also Christians.

"To understand Islam, we must go back to its founder, Mohammed, of the Quarish tribe in Mecca (AD570). An orphan, but in his youth came into contact with Jews and various groups of Christians. In the year AD610 an angel by the name of Jibrib appeared to Mohammed, and presented to him a god called Allah. At the age of 40 Mohammed began to preach his revelations of his god Allah, who was one of the many desert gods. Allah was the jackal god.

Mohammed preached and promoted this wilderness god to the same position as the God of the Jews and the Christians, he also saw himself as Allah's ultimate prophet!

The revelations that Mohammed wrote down during his angelic visitations are found in the Koran. Although Islam is an anti-religion, a contra-religion, written against Jewry and against Christendom, and in no-way reminiscent of the Judea-Christian revelation of the Lord. The character of the God of the bible bears no trace of similarity to the character of Allah, the god of Islam."[2]

True Revelation of God

When God created man, He set eternity in his heart. *"He has made everything beautiful in its time. He has also set eternity in the hearts of men" (Ecclesiastes 3:11).* When man sinned and fell, his concept of God became dim. He was, nevertheless, still able to appreciate God's existence in two ways: through nature and through his conscience *(see Romans 1:19-20 and Romans 2:14-15).*

If a man violates his conscience, his mind becomes darkened. Romans 1:21 tells us, *"For although they knew God, they neither glorified him as God nor gave thanks to him, but their thinking became futile and their foolish hearts were darkened."* The result of this darkening of the mind, the bible says, is the setting up of idols that are venerated and worshipped in place of the One True God *(see Romans 1:22-25).*

Idol Worship is Demonic

Behind these idols and their worship lie demonic powers. *"The sacrifices of pagans are offered to demons, not to God, and I do not want you to be participants with demons" (1 Corinthians 10:20).* "They sacrificed to demons, which are not God — gods they had not known, gods that recently appeared, gods your fathers did not fear" *(Deuteronomy 32:17).*

"The bible describes how sin and disobedience caused man to provide himself with false gods in order to satisfy his inherent religious craving. He tried to placate the unknown, the uncertain and the fearsome things around him; and above all, the threat of death. At the same time, the bible refers to man's longing for God, which is rooted deep in his conscience.

God then moved in this situation and revealed Himself to man. He imparted this revelation to the people of Israel. They were shown who He is, what He desires, and how man can come to Him. And God chose the people of Israel because he wanted to do so! This revelation was faithfully and meticulously written down in the bible for all of mankind, forever.

No one can approach God without this revelation. God's love is seen in His willingness and ability to reveal Himself to mankind. He gave His revelation to the children of Israel who were to steward and spread it.

In Romans 9:4 Paul says of the Jewish people, *'Theirs is the adoption as sons; theirs the divine glory, the covenants, the receiving of the law, the temple worship and the promises.'*

In other words, it was to them that God gave His revelation of Himself."[3]

❖

CHAPTER 10

Islam to the Attack

Muslims declare Israel Dead

On May 14th, 1948, Prime Minister Ben Gurion officially proclaimed a Jewish state under the name Israel. After nearly 2,000 years the Jews were now home again, just as God had promised!

"Return, faithless people," declares the Lord, "for I am your husband. I will choose one of you from every town and two from every clan and bring you to Zion.

(Jeremiah 3:14)

A state was at last a reality for the Jewish people, despite resistance. As the people celebrated their independence, Israel was plunged into war. The surroundings Arab states numbered some forty million inhabitants, and not one of them wanted a non-Muslim country as a neighbour.

The Shout from the Arabs was Clear

Death to the Jews and immediately attacked Israel in its infancy, anti-Semitism had been given a new face - Muslim anti-Zionism. Politicians throughout the world had declared Israel dead, giving it no chance.

Theologians in many circles proclaimed that modern Israel had nothing to do with ancient Israel. Replacement theology trained its sights on the tiny Jewish State. The Catholic Church refused to recognise the young State, and to this day the Vatican has never acknowledged Israel, because it sees itself as the new Israel and lays claim to its territory.

God however acknowledged Israel. He gathered the people, and He miraculously gave them their land.

Before she goes into labour, she gives birth; before the pains come upon her, she delivers a son. Who has ever heard of such a thing? Who has ever seen such things?

Can a country be born in a day or a nation be brought forth in a moment? Yet no sooner is Zion in labour than she gives birth to her children.

(Isaiah 66:7-8)

The prediction was that the Arabs would overrun it within weeks. Such overwhelming odds, how possibly could it cope, but it did. It survived and the Arabs were defeated. The Jews had returned to their land, never to leave it again.

I will plant Israel in their own land, never again to be uprooted from the land I have given them.

(Amos 9:15)

With the Jewish State officially proclaimed and installed, wave after wave of immigration followed and war followed war. After the War of Independence came the Suez Crisis, then the Six-Day War, the Yom Kippur War, the Lebanon War and, most recently, the Gulf War.

Not one of Israel's neighbours has made peace *(ex.: Egypt – Camp David Accord, as well as Qatar and Jordan – Express in 2006)* only hostilities and acts of aggression. In spite of this, Jews have returned to Israel by the thousands from all over the world.

But now, this is what the Lord says – he who created you, O Jacob, he who formed you, O Israel: "Fear not, for I have redeemed you; I have called you by name; you are mine.

When you pass through the waters, I will be with you; and when you pass through the rivers, they will not sweep over you. When you walk through the fire, you will not be burned; the flames will not set you ablaze.

For I am the Lord, your God, the Holy One of Israel, your Saviour; I give Egypt for your ransom, Cush and Seba in your stead. Since you are precious and honoured in my sight, and because I love you, I will give men in exchange for you, and people in exchange for your life.

Do not be afraid, for I am with you; I will bring your children from the east and gather you from the west. I will say to the north, 'Give them up!' and to the south, 'Do not hold them back.'

Bring my sons from afar and my daughters from the ends of the earth – everyone who is called by my name, whom I created for my glory, whom I formed and made."

(Isaiah 43:1-7)

Jewish immigrants have come from, North, South, East and West: Iran - Iraq - USA - Britain - France - Germany - South Africa - Yemen - Ethiopia and from Soviet Union.

"However, the days are coming," declares the Lord, "when men will no longer say, 'As surely as the Lord lives, who brought the Israelites up out of Egypt,' but they will say, 'As surely as the Lord lives, who brought the Israelites up out of the land of the north and out of all the countries where he had banished them.' For I will restore them to the land I gave their forefathers.

(Jeremiah 16:14-15)

The Last Word by Derek Prince

"By a decisive intervention of God in history: the re-gathering of the Jews in their own land. On May 14th 1948, after half a century of struggle, the modern State of Israel was born.

Of the countless prophecies in scripture that refer to the close of the present age, all without exception assume one thing: the presence of Israel as a Nation in their own land.

Until Israel was thus restored as a Nation, none of these prophecies could be fulfilled. Now the way is open for the fulfilment of them all.

> *Behold, I am going to make Jerusalem a cup that causes reeling to all the peoples around; and when the siege is against Jerusalem, it will also be against Judah.*
> *(Zechariah 12:2 NASB)*

Here is the first, immediate outcome of the formation of the State of Israel: a violent reaction by all the peoples around; resulting in a siege directed against both Jerusalem and Judah *(The Jewish People)*. Who are all the people around the State of Israel? Lebanon, Syria, Iraq, Jordan, Arabia, Egypt.

Clearly this first phase of the prophecy has already been fulfilled. As soon as the State of Israel came into being, all these nations immediately declared war on it and set out to annihilate it.

For two months, Jewish Jerusalem was besieged and was almost forced to capitulate through starvation. Upon this siege hung the destiny of all Judah *(the Jewish people in Israel)*.

Had Jewish Jerusalem fallen, the State of Israel would never have survived."[1]

❖

Europe's Part in the End Times (Chapter Update 2008)

Germany Capitulated

Pastor Joh. W. Matutis from the "Freie Nazareth-kirche e.V." (www.preach-in.de) in Berlin, Germany sent an email on the 24th July 2008, in writing he says:

I don't have to worry about Obama, but about the demonic spirit, that he will bring back home here from Berlin to the USA. Here in Berlin everything is occult and demonic. It seems – Obama comes to Berlin to fetch the blessing of the devil for himself. **Here is the "throne of Satan"** *(see Revelation 2:13-17).*

85

Obama will stand between the symbols of the gods Janus and Mercury and make his speech, for the Americans. He transfers not only pictures to America, he transfers from Berlin a demonic spirit from old Babylon etc. to the USA through his election campaign.

We Germans have suffered enough among these spirits. The country was divided for 70 years. So our country *(Germany)* and the town *(Berlin)* were under this curse.

In 1896/7 the "Pergamon Altar" was discovered:

- During this year there were the first Olympic Games in the modern times
- During this year the first Zionist-Congress took place
- During this year there was the first new outpouring of the Holy Spirit
- 50 years later the state of Israel was proclaimed
- 70 years later *(1967)* Jerusalem was taken by the Jews *(and after nearly 2,000 years Jerusalem was back in the hands of Jews)*

On the 9th of November, 1919 the German emperor resigns:

Germany capitulated. 70 years later, on the 9th of November, 1989 the Berlin Wall fell. The whole world was astonished – that this deadly wound was healed *(see Revelation 13:3,12,14)*.

Those of you **who understand biblical prophecy will know we are in the End-Times, the divine countdown is running!** We don't want this spirit of Pergamon to be transferred to the USA or the curse of God to be on the USA or the rest of the world, as it was over Germany and Europe *(first and second World War).*

The Brandenburg Gate and the Victory Column are dedicated to idols *(Janus and Mercury).*

Changing Laws to squeeze the Christian Church

"We are living in the days of the last Kingdom as prophesied by Daniel. We know the legs of Iron was the Roman Empire and the mixture of Iron and clay in the feet represent a collaboration between the last of the Roman Empire in the form of the Catholic Church and Europe.

By the Middle Ages Germanic Europe was known as the Holy Roman Empire and was dominated by what were called Prince Bishops, so that it was both a spiritual and a political power. Neither of those powers died, but today both have passed into the European Union through the 1957 Treaty of Rome.

> *Thou, O king, sawest, and behold a great image. This great image, whose brightness was excellent, stood before thee; and the form thereof was terrible. This image's head was of fine gold, his breast and his arms of silver, his belly and his thighs of brass, His legs of iron, his feet part of iron and part of clay.*
>
> *(Daniel 2:31-33 KJV)*

In Direct Opposition to God

Today Europe is setting itself up in direct opposition to God. Already we know the trouble the Church is having in France, Germany and Belgium. The Berlin Declaration in 1908 started the opposition to Christianity by declaring everything to do with the Holy Spirit was of the devil, thus committing the unpardonable sin.

With the First World War Germany slipped into depression during the 20's and 30's with the collapse of the bank bringing economic disaster. Germany and Old Europe was in turmoil but the time was right for the rise of a leader who would bring order to chaos and deliver them from their depression.

This was to be HITLER, backed by the Church his rise was phenomenal. His anti-Semitic values were born from the church at the time and his rise and rule was a type of Anti-Christ. He too will rise from a time of turmoil and depression, when people call out for a leader of vision and power, also backed by the Church. What does this have to do with Europe?

It is slowly changing laws to squeeze the Christian church out, and it makes no secret of this. To encourage support for the EU, the Council of Europe published a poster identifying Europe with the rebuilding of Babel!

Modelled on Pieter Bruegel's famous 16th century painting 'the Tower of Babel,' the poster shows the peoples of Europe rebuilding the tower that God destroyed in Genesis 11:5-9.

And the LORD came down to see the city and the tower, which the children of men builded. And the LORD said, Behold, the people is one, and they have all one language;

*and this they begin to do: and now nothing will be
restrained from them, which they have imagined to do.
Go to, let us go down, and there confound their language,
that they may not understand one another's speech. So the
LORD scattered them abroad from thence upon the face of
all the earth: and they left off to build the city.*

*Therefore is the name of it called Babel; because the LORD
did there confound the language of all the earth: and from
thence did the LORD scatter them abroad upon the face of
all the earth.*

(Genesis 11:5-9 KJV)

Note the statement shown on the poster 'Many Tongues
One Voice,' inverts God's judgement on Babel.

Note also that the normal European stars have been
inverted to a pentagram, which shows the horns, ears and
beard of Lucifer.

The man who designed it was inspired by the 12 stars
that in Catholic tradition halo the head of Mary. He still hopes
she will be incorporated into the design. So the actual flag is
of the 'Queen of Heaven' as the Queen of Europe, at the very
centre of the EU. After complaints by some Christians, it was
withdrawn. BUT in December 2000 they completed a new
EU Parliament building in Strasbourg in France. *(For access
to pictures online see reference in endnotes).*

A Woman Sitting on a Beast

But if you thought that was enough, that's not the end.
Even worse than the tower of Babel is the fact that they have

chosen another symbol to identify Europe, an image of a woman sitting on a beast - symbolic of both spiritual and political power!

There are two parliament buildings for Europe, one in Strasbourg in France, and the other in Brussels in Belgium - both contain murals depicting this woman. And outside the Council of Europe Building in Brussels is a crude sculpture of this evil, scarlet woman, riding the evil beast. Is she the woman referred to in Revelation 17?

This symbol of the European Union is printed on stamps, phone cards, and currency. The woman is known from Greek mythology as 'Europa' and literally she has been raped by the beast. Is that how the politicians see Europe?

"Rape of Europa"

Another symbol adopted by Europe, as curious as the Tower of Babel, is the Greek myth of the 'Rape of Europa.' This makes us ask - is Europe today being raped politically/financially/spiritually - and by whom? In every case a wanton woman, Europa, can be seen riding a beast *(Revelation 17:1-7)*, note especially from Revelation that the forehead of the woman riding the beast is branded with the name, 'Mystery Babylon.'

The mythical story is that Zeus, the father of the gods, spied Europa alone on the beach and lusted after her. He transformed himself into a bull of dazzling whiteness with horns like a crescent moon and lay down at her feet. She climbed on his back and he plunged with her into the waves of the sea before raping her.

Europa conceived a son, and after her death she received divine honours as 'Queen of Heaven,' whilst the bull dissolved into the constellation in the sky known as Taurus. Brussels and Strasbourg EU Parliaments both contain paintings of the woman on the beast.

A related issue may be the massive computer in Brussels called Euro Net, but nicknamed the 'Beast,' the first computer reputed, to be capable of storing personal data of the entire world population.

Is Europe the Babylon spoken of which will be destroyed in one hour *(Revelation 18:1-15)?*

And after these things I saw another angel come down from heaven, having great power; and the earth was lightened with his glory. And he cried mightily with a strong voice, saying, Babylon the great is fallen, is fallen, and is become the habitation of devils, and the hold of every foul spirit, and a cage of every unclean and hateful bird.

For all nations have drunk of the wine of the wrath of her fornication, and the kings of the earth have committed fornication with her, and the merchants of the earth are waxed rich through the abundance of her delicacies.

And I heard another voice from heaven, saying, Come out of her, my people, that ye be not partakers of her sins, and that ye receive not of her plagues. For her sins have reached unto heaven, and God hath remembered her iniquities.

Reward her even as she rewarded you, and double unto her double according to her works: in the cup which she hath filled fill to her double. How much she hath glorified herself, and lived deliciously, so much torment and sorrow give her: for she saith in her heart, I sit a queen, and am no widow, and shall see no sorrow. Therefore shall her plagues come in one day, death, and mourning, and famine; and she shall be utterly burned with fire: for strong is the Lord God who judgeth her.

And the kings of the earth, who have committed fornication and lived deliciously with her, shall bewail her, and lament for her, when they shall see the smoke of her burning, Standing afar off for the fear of her torment, saying, Alas, alas, that great city Babylon, that mighty city! for in one hour is thy judgment come.

And the merchants of the earth shall weep and mourn over her; for no man buyeth their merchandise any more: The merchandise of gold, and silver, and precious stones, and of pearls, and fine linen, and purple, and silk, and scarlet, and all thyine wood, and all manner vessels of ivory, and all manner vessels of most precious wood, and of brass, and iron, and marble, And cinnamon, and odours, and ointments, and frankincense, and wine, and oil, and fine flour, and wheat, and beasts, and sheep, and horses, and chariots, and slaves, and souls of men.

And the fruits that thy soul lusted after are departed from thee, and all things, which were dainty and goodly are departed from thee, and thou shalt find them no more at all.

The merchants of these things, which were made rich by her, shall stand afar off for the fear of her torment, weeping and wailing.

(Revelation 18:1-15 KJV)

The Seat of Satan

The gigantic 'Altar of Pergamon' dominates Germany's Pergamon Museum in former East Berlin.

Originally sited in Asia Minor, the Temple at Pergamon with its altar was the centre of Emperor Worship; the price of refusal to acknowledge the Emperor as God - ritual murder on the altar! Revelation 2:13 calls it 'Satan's Seat' or '"The Throne of Satan.'

> *And to the angel of the church in Pergamos write; These things saith he which hath the sharp sword with two edges; I know thy works, and where thou dwellest, even where Satan's seat is: and thou holdest fast my name, and hast not denied my faith, even in those days wherein Antipas was my faithful martyr, who was slain among you, where Satan dwelleth.*
>
> *(Revelation 2:12-13 KJV)*

On its steps early Christians were martyred for their unswerving faith in Christ. German archaeologist Carl Humann found it in almost perfect condition in the late 1800's and carefully shipped every stone to Berlin. In 1902 Kaiser Wilhelm II celebrated its erection in Berlin as the 'proudest monument to his reign' - with an extravagant festival to the pagan gods!

It is significant that within a short time of this, the history of Germany was to be dominated by a sequence of events, which could only be attributed to satanic control. Yet another relic from the past is the Ishtar Gate again brought back to

Germany stone by stone, it was said to be one of the gates into Babylon and originally had around it 337 images of the dragon god. Today you can still see some of the images. 337 in numerology is the number of sheol or hell. These gates to the occult represent the entrance or gates to hell.

You can clearly see the images of the dragon god, lovingly restored to its former glory. Why would they bring two items like this, which speak of evil and have connections with Satan? Europe is becoming a Godless organisation whose intentions are far from righteous. Will the Anti-Christ come up through the countries of Europe and use them to fight Christ at his return? Don't forget we are not looking for 10 countries now to fulfil the prophecy but 10 Kings then who have power for an hour. No matter how many countries join the EU there is no telling what will happen in the future and how Europe will be divided or Kingdomised in the future for the purpose and will of the Anti-Christ.

We should think long and hard as British Christians before entering the EU. It is not a matter of losing our pound but losing our right and freedom to be a Christian, to worship as and when we please. Europe will be punished for its stand against God, would we want to be a part of that?"[1]

❖
Endnotes

Preface

1. Appointment in Jerusalem, by Derek and Lydia Prince, Publisher: Chosen Books, Zondervan Publishing House, USA, 1975, p174

Chapter 3 Babylonian Captivity of the Church

1. Kyrkan och Synagogan, by Bernhard Blumenkranz, p21

2. The Gospel According to Rome, by James G. McCarthy, ISBN-13: 978-1565071070, Publisher: Harvest House Pub, 1995

3. The Gospel According to Rome

4. The Gospel According to Rome

5. Prince of Darkness, Antichrist and The New World Order, by Grant R. Jeffrey, ISBN: 0-921714-04-1, Publisher: Forntier Research Publications, Canada, 1994, p228-229

6. Newsweek: December 11, 1989, Super Partners - An Ambitious Game Plan for a New Era, Volume CXIV, No. 24, Publisher: Newsweek Inc., 1989

Chapter 4 Replacement Theology Produces Anti-Semitism

1. Kyrkan och Synagogan, by Wilhelm Maurer, p56

Chapter 5 Jewish Migrants are Waving the Flag

1. Christ or Mohammed? The Bible or The Koran?, by F.S. Copleston, ISBN-13: 978-1871703009, Publisher: Nuprint Ltd. UK, 1989

Chapter 6 The Rise of Modern Zionism

1. The Rebirth of the State of Israel, by Arthur W. Kac, Publisher: Moody Press, USA, 1958

2. The Rebirth of the State of Israel

Chapter 7 Moses Hess the Activist

1. "Der Judenstaat" (The Jewish State), by Theodor Herzl, First published in Vienna, 1896, The first English-language edition, was translated by Sylvie d'Avigdor, and published by Nutt, London, England, 1896

Chapter 9 Mohammed was not a True Prophet

1. Christ or Mohammed? The Bible or The Koran?, by F.S. Copleston, ISBN-13: 978-1871703009, Publisher: Nuprint Ltd. UK, 1989

2. The Jews, People of The Future, by Ulf Ekman, ISBN-10: 91-7866-210-9, Publisher: Word of Life Publications, Sweden, 1993, p86

3. The Jews, People of The Future, p87-88

Chapter 10 Islam to the Attack

1. Appointment in Jerusalem, by Derek and Lydia Prince, Publisher: Chosen Books, Zondervan Publishing House, USA, 1975, p179-180

Chapter 11 Europe's Part in the End Times (Chapter Update 2008)

1. Taken from: www.thewatcher.co.uk, Article link: http://docs.wixstatic.com/ugd/257507_8acffb80d9224ac599ee8b2c73d28009.pdf, also see the Ministry of David Hathaway: www.propheticvision.org.uk

Bible translations

- Unless otherwise indicated, all scriptural quotations are from the HOLY BIBLE, NEW INTERNATIONAL VERSION ®. NIV ®. Copyright © 1973, 1978, 1984 by the International Bible Society. Used by permission of Zondervan Publishing House. All rights reserved.

- Scripture references marked KJV are taken from the King James Version of the bible.

- Scripture marked NASB are taken from the New American Standard Bible®, Copyright © 1960, 1962, 1963, 1968, 1971, 1972,

1973, 1975, 1977, 1995 by The Lockman Foundation. Used by permission.

- Scripture references marked NKJV are taken from the New King James Version®. Copyright © 1982 by Thomas Nelson, Inc. Used by permission. All rights reserved.

- Strong, James. S.T.D., L.L.D. 1890. Strong's Exhaustive Concordance, Dictionaries (Lexicon) of the Hebrew and Greek Words.

❖

Recommended Reading

- Ad Diem Illum Laetissimum, No14, by Pope Pius X
- Battle for Israel, by Lance Lambert
- Bless Israel for God's Sake, by Sven Nilsson
- Building a People of Power, by Ian Andrews
- Egyptian Religion, by Sir Wallis Budge
- Everyday Life in Babylonia and Assyria, by H.W.F. Saggs
- Fantasy Explosion, by Bob Maddux
- From Rock to Rock, by Eric Barger
- Growing in the Prophetic, by Mike Bickle with Michael Sullivant
- High-Lights of the Bible, by Ray C. Stedman
- Magnae Dei Matris, by Pope Leo XII
- Munificentissimus Deus, No20, by Pope Pius XII
- New Age to New Birth, by Roy and Rae Livesey
- Pagans and Christians, by Robin Lane Fox
- Prophecy Past and Present, by Clifford Hill
- Reflections on the Christ, by David Spangler
- Second Vatican Council, Dogmatic Constitution on the Church, No59

- Spiritual Mysteries Revealed!, by Morris Cerullo
- The Church of the Living God, by Ulf Ekman
- The God of Ecstasy, by Arthur Evans
- The Lion Handbook of the Bible
- The Mystery Religions, by S. Angus
- The New Cults, by Walter Martin
- The Plan and its Implementation, by M.E. Hazelhurst
- The Prophetic Ministry, by Ulf Ekman
- The Veneration of Mary; Our Lady of Perpetual Help; Our Lady of Perpetual Succor, by Pope Pius IX (compare these scriptures: Hebrews 7:25; Hebrews 13:5-6)
- The Women's Encyclopedia of Myths and Secrets, by Barbara Walker
- Toward a World Religion for the New Age, by Lola Davis
- Women's Dionysian Initiation, by Linda Fierz-David
- Wycliffe Bible Encyclopedia

❖

Ministry Profile

Doctor Alan Pateman, an apostle, is the President and Founder of **"Alan Pateman Ministries International"** (APMI), which was established in England back in 1987, a Christian-based *(parachurch)* non-profit and non-denominational outreach. This ministry is now focusing in two main areas: First **"Connecting for Excellence"** Apostolic Networking (CFE) and secondly, the teaching arm, **"LifeStyle International Christian University"** (LICU).

CFE is a multi-facetted missions organisation with the purpose of connecting leaders for divine opportunities and building lasting relationships, to touch the lives of leaders literally the world over. Apostle Dr Alan Pateman has to date ordained more than 500 ministers in over 50 NATIONS. In addition there are ministries, churches and schools who are in Association or Affiliation, looking to him for apostolic counsel and oversight.

Secondly LICU, which was founded in 2007, is a study program to help people discover their purpose and destiny. A global network of university campuses and correspondence students, demonstrating the Supernatural Kingdom of God through Doctrinal, Apostolic and Prophetic Teaching. Dr Alan holds the position of President/CEO, Professor of Theology, Biblical Studies and Apostolic Ministry. LICU is exploding throughout Europe, Asia and Africa, enhancing the Body of Christ

Dr Alan has authored more than 35 books including numerous teaching materials and LICU university courses (30) along with hundreds of Truth for the Journey articles on kingdom lifestyle *(that are regularly distributed globally via the internet).*

He is recognised as an Apostle, Bishop, Leadership Mentor, University Educator, Motivational Speaker, Connector and Author, who has also been featured on national and international TV and radio networks throughout the years.

Currently Apostle Alan, his wife Dr Jennifer reside in Lucca *(Tuscany)* Italy and travel out from their Apostolic Company.

- Alan Pateman Ph.D., D.Min., D.D., M.A., B.Th.

Academic Background

Dr. Alan Pateman attended several colleges throughout his training *(including studying Theology at Roffey Place, Horsham, UK and a Member of Kerygma - with Rev. Colin Urquhart and Dr. Bob Gordon - 1985-1987)* before being awarded a Doctorate of Divinity *(2006)* in recognition of his lifetime achievements by the International College of Excellence, now "DanEl Christian College" *(President: Dr. Robb Thompson USA)* also "Life Christian University" *(Dr. Douglas Wingate USA)* where he also earned a Bachelor of Theology B.Th. *(2006),* a Master of Arts in Theology M.A., a Doctor of Ministry in Theology D.Min., *(2007)* and Doctor of Philosophy in Theology Ph.D. *(2013)* from LICU.

❖

To Contact the Author

Please email:

Alan Pateman Ministries International

Email: apostledr@alanpateman.com
Web: www.AlanPatemanMinistries.com

*Please include your prayer requests
and comments when you write.*

❖

Other Books

Healing and Deliverance, A Present Reality

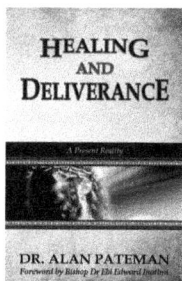

Within the pages of this book (which has to be a "must-read" for any serious enquirer into the Healing and Deliverance Ministry), Dr. Alan unfolds a different pathway, so that the heartbeat of God's message of God's total deliverance can be released into the church of Jesus Christ today.

ISBN: 978-1-909132-80-1, Pages: 188, Format: Paperback, First Print: 1994
Also available in eBook format!

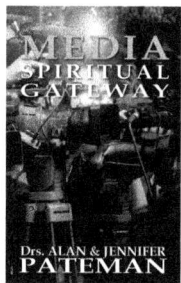

Media, Spiritual Gateway

Let's face it; we live in the era of fake news! It's always existed, but never been quite so prominent. Today it's an all-out-war between fact and political fiction. The media has been sabotaged by political activism. Gone are the days of impartiality and objective unbiased reporting, with many sources saying that true journalism is dead.

ISBN: 978-1-909132-54-2, Pages: 192, Format: Paperback, Published: 2018
Also available in eBook format!

Truth for the Journey Books

Millennial Myopia, From a Biblical Perspective

The standard for every generation is Jesus. However Millennial Myopia describes the trap of focusing everything on one particular generation or demographic cohort, at the exclusion and expense of all others. The Church cannot afford to make this mistake too. Loaded with research, this book takes readers on a journey of discovery, revealing the true nature of kingdom diversity.

ISBN: 978-1-909132-67-2, Pages: 216, Format: Paperback, Published: 2017
Also available in eBook format!

The Age of Apostolic Apostleship Complete Series

In order to view how the Apostolic baton was successfully passed from one generation to the next. Knowing that through the perseverance and obedience of others - history as we know it was altered forever. Dr. Alan Pateman, a modern day apostle (ascension) looks to reflect on their testimony in this wonderful book.

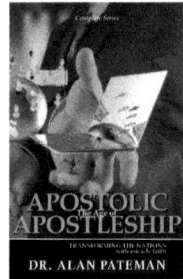

ISBN: 978-1-909132-65-8, Pages: 420
Format: Paperback, Published: 2017
Also available in eBook format!

TONGUES, Our Supernatural Prayer Language

In writing to the church at Corinth, Paul encouraged them to continue the practice of speaking with other tongues in their worship of God and in their prayer lives as a means of spiritual edification. "He that speaketh in an unknown tongue edifies, charges, builds himself up like a battery."

ISBN: 978-1-909132-44-3, Pages: 144, Format: Paperback, Published: 2016
Also available in eBook format!

Dear Friends,

Have you considered becoming one of our international students? We are privileged to welcome you, from around the world, to "LifeStyle International Christian University" *(the teaching arm of Alan Pateman Ministries International).* **An English speaking university** dedicated to your success; to see you trained and equipped to fully succeed in your God given Destiny.

It is our passion to raise up the leaders of tomorrow, who will have influence in all realms of authority, including the Body of Christ. Men and women of strategy, wisdom and true godliness, who'll stand with stature and maturity in this hour.

It's undeniable that in today's world, recognised education has become indispensable, therefore it is our desire to offer well balanced and well structured courses. Those that have been written by gifted and talented ministers of God, who seek to be inspired by God's Holy Spirit.

Consequently we have put together a **flexible curriculum,** designed both for correspondence students and campuses, which is a strategy to reach the distant learner; whether provincial, national or international. In fact we have many correspondence students from around the world, including a growing number of successful campuses, in various countries.

This is a growing platform, where men and women of dignity and passion, can grow and be established in their God given endeavours. As God is the healer of the nations, we pray and believe that many of our alumni will go on to **become world changers** in their own right.

We are proud of each and every one of our LICU students.
It would be our pleasure if you would join them on this incredible journey!

Doctor Alan Pateman

Alan Pateman Prof. Ph.D., D.Min., D.D., M.A., B.Th.
PRESIDENT AND CEO
www.licuuniversity.com www.cfeapostolicnetwork.com
Email: info@licuuniversity.com   Mob: +39 366 329 1315

For more information visit our website/facebook or contact our office, using the details below:

Website: www.licuuniversity.com
Facebook: www.facebook.com/LICUMainCampus
Email: info@licuuniversity.com
Telephone: +39 366 329 1315

Alan Pateman Ministries
Presents

Conference

CONNECTING FOR
EXCELLENCE Lucca
Italy

An international apostolic
and prophetic network

YOUR HOSTS: ALAN PATEMAN   JENNIFER PATEMAN

apostledr@alanpateman.com, Tel. 0039 366 329 1315
WWW.ALANPATEMANMINISTRIES.COM

Please contact our office or download the registration form.
Registration fee: €40

All Books Available

at

APMI PUBLICATIONS

Email: publications@alanpateman.com
*Also Available from Amazon.com
and other retail outlets.*

*If you purchased this book through Amazon.com
or other and enjoyed reading it, or perhaps one of
my other books, I would be grateful if you could
take a couple of minutes to write a Customer
Review, many thanks.*

www.ingramcontent.com/pod-product-compliance
Lightning Source LLC
Chambersburg PA
CBHW071607040426
42452CB00008B/1269